Think and Get Paid

Think and Get Paid

Evie Lawson

EV Publishing LLC

Contents

Dedication — viii

Think and Get Paid — 1
CHAPTER 2 — 5
CHAPTER 3 — 7
CHAPTER 4 — 10
CHAPTER 5 — 12
CHAPTER 6 — 16
CHAPTER 7 — 18
CHAPTER 8 — 20
CHAPTER 9 — 22
CHAPTER 10 — 25
CHAPTER 11 — 27
CHAPTER 12 — 31
CHAPTER 13 — 35
CHAPTER 14 — 37
CHAPTER 15 — 40

About the Author 48
Book Description 49

Copyright © 2021 by Evie Lawson

All rights reserved. No part of this book may be reproduced in any manner whatsoever without written permission except in the case of brief quotations embodied in critical articles and reviews.

First Printing, 2021

This book is dedicated to the brave members of the armed forces

Think and Get Paid

By
Evie Lawson
BA, MBA

CHAPTER 1
INTRODUCTION

Think and get paid is a simple, straightforward statement, yet these words are powerful enough to change anyone's life who believes and acts on its message. Earth provides a large abundance of evidence proving that energy directed towards a specific goal inevitably manifests itself into realization. The recently mentioned statement is not just a belief but a scientific fact. Numerous psychologists have stated that "the mind is the most powerful tool man has at their disposal." A human being can literally think and get paid or whatever else they may desire to acquire.

Thinking is the most essential and fundamental component of obtaining whatever one wants. However, there are also general principles an individual must employ to achieve the physical realization of the desire. The author will describe these principles in great detail throughout this book. The author will also explain these life-changing principles and their features and instructions in an easy-to-understand and practical manner.

A single concrete idea is all that is required to attain prosperity. The principles expressed in this text contain the most beneficial and effective means of conceiving sound ideas and then putting them into practical action.

When you start thinking and getting paid, you will recognize that wealth begins with a state of mind, amidst recognition of specific goals, with little or no hard labor. Almost every individual in the world is fascinated by how the rich and famous have acquired their fame and fortune. The author is no different. Because of this curiosity, the author spent numerous years researching and analyzing more than five hundred of the most successful people worldwide to determine how they transformed their conceived goals into reality. Without such examination, the author could not have composed this text.

The information presented in this text is life-changing. There is no doubt that as soon as you comprehend these profound instructions and start applying the appropriate actions needed to attain your specific goals, your financial situation will begin improving. Even though the recently mentioned statement may sound unconventional, you must not think this is impossible because it is, in fact, possible. One of humanity's chief flaws is the doubt that creeps into their mind when faced with a situation that takes the person out of their comfort zone. Even if there are numerous examples of individuals who have achieved success in their respective professions, much of humanity feels like they have no control of their lives. These individuals truly believe the undesirable situation they are in is impossible to get out of, and anything they do is bound to fail. That belief is not valid. The author wrote this book for individuals who believe that success leaves clues and inquires to understand the actions and thought patterns that made millions of people successful throughout history.

Success befalls the individuals who come to be success-conscious. The same adage can be said about failure. Failure happens to the folks who inadequately permit themselves to believe they are failures. This text strives to encourage all who inquire to discover the art of controlling their hazardous thoughts and live the life they were meant to live. Think and Get Paid is about informing readers that we all are the Masters of our Fate, the Captains of our Souls because we possess the capability to manage our thoughts.

This text will help the reader appreciate why our brains become magnetized with the dominating thoughts that we retain in our subconscious and draw the forces, the individuals, and life occurrences that correspond with our dominating thoughts' quality.

While engaging with this text, it is essential to maintain an open mind. Recognize, as you read, these are proven principles derived from a wide variety of successful individuals. This information is factual, and with the proper action, your entire financial fortune will change forever.

CHAPTER 2

Desire

To accomplish any worthwhile endeavor, one must desire to achieve the task. You can call it ambition, desire, passion, or hunger, whatever the term you want to use; if you do not possess this trait, it will be challenging to transform a specific goal into its physical realization. Once you have decided on a well-defined goal, it is beneficial to place all your energy, willpower, and effort towards attaining that goal.

Successful individuals are successful because they wanted to obtain success more than anything else. They created a plan to accomplish that objective after implementing a dominating obsession in their minds. The man or woman who desires to live a financially independent life does not allow the idea of failure to dwell in their mind. Instead, they fill their minds with the desire to receive adequate compensation. Desiring wealth with a state of mind that displays an obsession, then devising definite plans and means to earn wealth, and supporting those plans with a tenacity that does not acknowledge failure, will undoubtedly bring riches.

One of the best methods to transfer your desire into its

monetary equivalent is to follow a detailed list of proven steps. These steps are as follows:

-First, determine in your imagination the precise amount of wealth you desire.

-Second, define what you propose to provide in return for the wealth you covet.

-Third, set a specific date regarding when you plan to control the wealth you want.

-Fourth, devise a well-defined plan to attain your goal and begin putting this strategy into action.

-Fifth, compose an exact, brief text describing the number of funds you expect to obtain, specify the period for its acquisition, explain what you aim to provide in return for the funds, and specify the procedure you will employ to accumulate it.

-Sixth, express your composed statement audibly, twice every day, once before sleeping and once after you wake up. It is critical to visualize yourself already in possession of the funds while you read.

Individuals who exclusively display wealth consciousness regularly acquire vast fortunes. Wealth consciousness suggests that the subconscious has become so thoroughly immersed with the passion for wealth that one can perceive oneself already in ownership of it.

These directions may appear absurd to the doubter, but a vast amount of evidence proves these guidelines work. It may also be beneficial for the reader to recognize that these directions did not solely come from the author. However, the successful individuals the author analyzed expressed the measures they took to obtain success, and the recently mentioned actions were the exact strategy used.

CHAPTER 3

BELIEF

Faith is a quintessential emotion, especially for individuals who desire success and wealth. This belief is true because, in a situation where faith is mixed with the vibration of thought, the subconscious mind immediately recognizes the thought, transforms it into its spiritual equivalent, and transmits it to the Universal Energy. Prayer with conceived faith is an illustration of this point. A person who believes they can be whatever they want to be will exactly live that particular lifestyle.

Faith is undoubtedly one of the most influential positive emotions because of its capability to dictate thought vibration. Belief in a specific outcome immediately enters the subconscious mind, where it is converted into its spiritual realization. This process is the only way one can communicate with Universal Energy.

The best tactic to induce faith is to appropriate positive affirmations or recited instructions to the subconscious mind. This process is called self-suggestion. The practice of self-suggestion will enable you to influence your subconscious mind in a manner that will allow you to believe you will obtain the object of your desire. Following that process, your subconscious mind will give you the feeling of faith, and your actions will be directed towards securing that which you desire.

The author understands that faith is a controversial topic that is difficult to articulate because it is a state of mind that is intangible and developed over time. Nevertheless, this emotion is real, and repeated affirmations to the subconscious can produce faith. Any thought emotionalized and infused with faith works promptly to transmute itself into its tangible equivalent or counterpart. The feeling portion of thoughts is vital because the subconscious does not know the difference between a positive or opposing idea, and improper use of faith can lead to hazardous outcomes. This means the subconscious mind will transpose into its tangible equivalent, a thought vibration of a dangerous or unfavorable reality, just as quickly as it will act upon thought notions of a positive or valuable quality.

Numerous people all around the world believe they are destined to live a life of poverty and discomfort. They believe their life is out of their control, but the truth is that they are the producers of their troubles because of their negative feelings. The author can not stress the importance of replacing the feelings and beliefs of failure with the emotion of faith enough. Your variety of faith is the component that commands the performance of your subconscious mind. Nothing prevents an individual from tricking their subconscious mind. It is not an impossible task to entertain thoughts of prosperity and happiness, even if the current situation is far from ideal.

You can not obtain a high level of faith overnight. Still, belief in oneself is adequately acquired when the individual utilizes the capability to incorporate faith with any thought sent to the subconscious mind with a conscious effort and practice.

Readers of this text should comprehend a tremendous distinction between hoping for something and being prepared to receive something. No person is ready to accept anything until the person truly believes it can be acquired. The individual who wants to succeed in life must constantly display a belief method, not wishful thinking. Open-mindedness is necessary for one to develop belief, encourage faith, determination, and self-assurance. It is no more challenging to aim high in life than to allow despair and hardship to overtake one's lifestyle.

CHAPTER 4

SELF-SUGGESTION

Self-suggestion is a phrase that pertains to every intrapersonal suggestion and any directed incentive which encompasses one's mind through the senses. In simpler terms, self-suggestion are the thoughts a person attempts to think on purpose. An example would be a basketball player silently telling his or herself repeatedly they will make the jump shot during shooting practice.

In general, the thoughts created by the application of auto-suggestion deliberately reach and influences the subconscious mind. The thoughts can be positive or negative; the subconscious does not discriminate.

The Universe has created humans to possess the ability to have complete control over the substances that influence the subconscious mind. However, numerous people do not make productive use of this power, and a wide variety does not even know they have this power.

Self-Suggestion gives every individual the capability to control what they allow to enter the subconscious mind. These thoughts can be creative or, by negligence, ideas of a negative influence. This is why you must use positive repetition of affirmations when attempting to influence your subconscious mind. Also, applying emotion to your self-suggested affirmations will increase your chances of attaining noticeable results because the thoughts sent to the subconscious will be emotionalized with belief.

Discouragement may attempt to creep into your mind when initially attempting to guide and direct your self-suggestions. You may feel like you are wasting time or is doing something unnecessary. However, it is vital to realize that positively reaching and influencing your subconscious mind will increase your chances of achieving financial and personal success.

Your capacity to utilize the practice of self-suggestion will depend considerably upon your ability to focus on a specific goal till your desire to accomplish that goal becomes an overwhelming obsession.

The subconscious mind collects any command transmitted in a feeling of unadulterated faith; however, the commands must be manifested frequently through repetition before the unconscious mind understands them and hands over to you practical plans for actualizing the command. When the subconscious presents a plan, it is imperative to put the plan into action immediately. In the situation where the plans arise, they will seemingly flash within your mind in the manner of inspiration. Act upon the inspiration as promptly as you experience it; omission to do this will be disastrous to your progress.

CHAPTER 5

RELEVANT KNOWLEDGE

"Knowledge is power," a motto we all have heard at one time or another. Even though this phrase is familiar, the real meaning behind the words is not as relatable. Before we dive into the "knowledge is power" proverb, let us first define the varieties of knowledge relevant to thinking and getting paid. For this text, we will examine two classifications of knowledge which are general and specialized. General knowledge is the primary education a student receives while in high school and elementary. This type of information has minimal value in acquiring wealth. An illustration of this statement can be found within college universities and high schools. These educators have acquired a wide assortment of information, but most earn a small amount of money. They specialize in education, but they do not specialize in the fundamentals of accumulating wealth.

Before we go any further, let us acknowledge a common misconception. The universal belief that knowledge alone will attract wealth is not valid. Knowledge obtained through educational institutions will not attract an abundance of wealth unless the specified knowledge is incorporated and effectively managed, through tangible forms of action, to an inevitable end of wealth accumulation. In other words, getting a degree alone will not bring financial success. However, an individual's efforts to put that acquired knowledge into beneficial action through a well-devised plan will lead to funds' attainment. Lack of comprehension of the recently mentioned statement has denoted the cause of confusion for individuals who believe knowledge is power. The fact is that knowledge is merely potential power. It converts power exclusively when made into tangible methods of action and directed to a substantive purpose.

Countless people make the error of believing that because various celebrities, musicians, athletes, and other personalities did not finish school or go to college, knowledge is not important at all, but this is not true. They may not have needed a conventional education to succeed, but they have acquired a genius-level of specialized knowledge in their particular professions. This misconception emanates from the lack of comprehension regarding the meaning of the word "educate." That term originated from the Latin expression "educate," meaning obtaining, drawing out, and developing from inside. An educated person does not perpetually have to obtain an excess of conventional knowledge to be considered educated. An educated person is an individual who has learned how to utilize the abilities of their mind in a manner that allows that individual to acquire anything they desire. A person is educated when they comprehend where to get knowledge when needed and how to assemble that knowledge into tangible action strategies.

Let us discuss another type of knowledge. Specialized knowledge is relevant, logical, efficient, or vital information regarding a specific occupation or profession. Individuals utilize this type of education to learn the profession and its interconnectedness. It is any information that pertains to a specific trade, job, or skill. An illustration of a person acquiring specialized knowledge is a chess player learning all the chess rules and regulations. Unlike general knowledge, specialized knowledge can drastically affect one's financial situation.

The ambitious individual can achieve monetary independence through specialized knowledge by first deciding the specialized knowledge needed and the goal it requires, mainly a primary aim. Once you have determined your primary goal, the following action should be locating accurate information involving trustworthy learning sources. As relevant information is acquired, organization and utilization for a well-defined purpose through sound strategies must be implemented to realize your primary goal.

Prosperous folks, within numerous professions, never cease obtaining specialized knowledge linked to their primary goal, trade, or occupation. The people who are not as successful as they would like to be regularly commit the error of assuming that the learning phase concludes when one completes school. The truth is that conventional schooling produces little more than to place a person in the course of discovering how to obtain valuable knowledge.

In conclusion, there is never an established fee for solid ideas! It does not cost a dime to conceive a world-changing idea for a product or service. There will always be a universal demand for the person capable of uncovering solutions to the numerous unfavorable predicaments human beings encounter daily. Specialized knowledge can not only change one person's circumstances but can positively affect countless individuals all around the world.

CHAPTER 6

IMAGINATION

Imagination is a faculty of an individual's mind that can generate mental images of something unreal or produce innovative and creative ideas. The imagination is where the majority of history's most extraordinary ideas have been conceived. It is a fact that humans can produce anything imagined. The skeptical reader can find proof of the recently mentioned statement by analyzing how humans have discovered and harnessed nature's capabilities throughout the preceding two thousand years and the human race's complete history. The millions of inventions, products, and services produced by man speak for themselves.

For this principle, we will examine two contrasting forms of imagination, creative and synthetic. Synthetic imagination is the faculty of one's mind that arranges traditional theories, facts, or designs into brand-new combinations. This type of imagination does not create anything; it simply manages the substance of expertise, literacy, and research with which it is supplied. Synthetic imagination is practiced mainly by the inventor and scientist. The other form of imagination is creative imagination. Through this faculty of the mind, the individual has firsthand contact with the universal energy. This particular mental platform is where intuitive ideas and revelations are obtained. Through creative imagination, one can receive thought vibrations from another mind in a manner that allows the individual to harmonize or interact with other people's subconscious minds. This type of imagination primarily operates when the conscious mind fluctuates rapidly, usually when the conscious mind is aroused through an influential desire. The distinguished personalities of business, trade, economics, celebrated actors, composers, lyricists, and authors became exceptional because they utilized creative imagination.

Both forms of imagination become more valuable with application and practice, exactly like a muscle or organ. Desire is simply a thought, a notion, and the most beneficial emotion one may attain. The same sentiment can be stated about imagination; it has no use unless unrelenting action is placed behind making the object of the imagination tangible. While synthetic imagination will be utilized most regularly in transforming the notion of desire into wealth, it is beneficial to be aware of the predicaments that require creative imagination. Your imaginative faculty may have come to be limited because of inaction; however, imagination can be improved and made alert with deliberate practice.

It is essential to make efficient utilization of imagination because ideas are the source of any prosperity. Prosperous thoughts and lifestyles are the results of imagination. The universal energy will always have the back of the person who recognizes precisely what they want and is strong-minded enough to do whatever it takes to achieve the goal.

CHAPTER 7

ORGANIZED PLANNING

Organized planning utilizes rational, well-organized, and methodical schemes to suffice objectives and accomplish goals. Thoughtful planning is required for achievement in any endeavor intended to acquire wealth. Organized planning denotes an individual's motivation for establishing specific goals and what particular tasks are needed to reach those goals.

There are several vital aspects of organized planning: strategic, tactical, operational, and contingency. The strategic element outlines the essential goals that encompass an individual's purpose or primary aim. The tactical aspect specifies how one will execute the strategic objective. This particular aspect includes specific short-term goals that uphold the overall objective. The operational element incorporates what the individual needs to do daily to accomplish the relevant goals. Last is the contingency plan. This aspect is a set of actions that will be taken when a disaster or unexpected emergency occurs. Contingency procedures incorporate a vast spectrum of potential predicaments and proper responses for external circumstances that could negatively affect goal achievement.

This paragraph is an excellent place to address what to do when met with obstacles while executing an organized plan. It is vital to acknowledge the possibility of the first plan not working. In this circumstance, it is imperative not to get discouraged but instead reinstate that plan with a brand-new plan; if this latest plan is unsuccessful, substitute it with another until a strategy that does work is discovered. Persistence is critical when attempting to achieve prosperity, and the difference between the individuals who are prosperous from the one who is not is their will to win. When a plan is unsuccessful, that momentary setback is not a permanent defeat, it may simply indicate the plan is not as practical as required.

A person's success can be no more essential than their plans are solid. A person is never considered a quitter until they quit in their mind. Everybody admires the individuals who have amassed wealth but does not acknowledge the temporary setbacks these people had to overcome before achieving prosperity. When disappointment happens, receive it as a sign that the plans are not as dependable as first thought, reconstruct the strategy, and start from the beginning working toward the achievement of the primary goal. Do not give up; the universal energy is on your side.

CHAPTER 8

DECISION MAKING

A survey was conducted in which twenty thousand men and women were asked why they felt like they did not achieve all of their inspired goals. The overwhelming answer to this question was procrastination. This analysis proves a worldwide fact that procrastination is one of the main reasons why millions of the most incredible ideas and inventions are in the countless graveyards of the world.

Likewise, an examination of the individuals who had amassed vast prosperity confessed that one of the main reasons they could accumulate the desired wealth was the practice of making decisions quickly and adjusting those choices gradually if required. Folks who are unsuccessful in acquiring sufficient funds possess the habit of making decisions rather slowly or not at all and reversing those choices rapidly.

Another factor that influences procrastination in decision-making regarding acquiring satisfactory compensation is the opinions of other people. These individuals allow the fear of criticism to dictate their decision making which can lead to hazardous circumstances.

It is crucial not to allow others' opinions to influence decision-making because you will not possess any intrapersonal desire. Only the opinions of the people in complete agreement and unanimity with the attainment of your primary goal should matter, and even then, you have to think for yourself. The recently mentioned statement also goes for comrades and families. The reasoning being their beliefs can handicap one through opinions and contempt. Countless people bear inadequacy fixations throughout life because some individual damaged their self-confidence through judgments or contempt.

The usefulness of decisiveness depends on the bravery needed to make conflicting decisions. More often than not, in the history of humanity, meaningful choices were influenced by meaningful opportunities.

For the individual who has been burdened with the habit of indecision, there is hope. This trait only becomes permanent if one allows it to through the negligence of controlling their thoughts. It is not difficult to quickly decide on something, nor is it difficult to not depend on other people's opinions. The habit of not making discerned decisions promptly can influence a person to live a life of uncertainty and disappointment.

The individual who will do everything in their mental capacity to prioritize making decisive decisions will dictate their economic freedom and lifestyle. Just trust and believe in yourself when making a decision and if you are wrong, make a better decision the next go around. You possess an intellect and cognizance of your own. Do not forget to use it, and reach your own decisions.

CHAPTER 9

PERSISTENCE

Persistence is a necessary trait to possess when attempting to convert desire into its tangible realization. In order to adequately utilize the power of persistence, one must maintain an incredible amount of willpower. The men and women who acquire immense prosperity display a consistent amount of willpower, and persistence to ensure their goals' achievements.

The difference between the person who lives a life of prosperity from those who do not is that the person who has obtained prosperity did not give up when met with temporary setbacks. Instead, their desire to achieve their goals was so significant that failure was not an option in their minds. This statement illustrates why the negligence of persistence is one of the notable causes of poverty and unhappiness. If a reader of this text knows they give up whenever met with setbacks, do not stress about it. This deficiency can be corrected by focusing on and unapologetically working towards attaining a primary goal. Yes, the lack of persistence and willpower can be fixed with consistent effort. Persistence is a disposition of thought and can be developed.

Like other emotions of thoughts, persistence is based upon distinct elements, including clarification of one's primary goal, ambition, confidence, organization of plans, relevant information, willpower, and habits.

The lack of finances becomes a person's reality when they do not believe they are worthy of possessing finances. If one does not consistently focus on attaining funds, one will be subjected to a lifestyle of disappointment both financially and emotionally. The previously mentioned statement is why persistence is so important. With persistence, one can constantly work towards accomplishing one's primary goal, thus focusing on a positive outcome instead of letting one's mind drift towards a negative outcome. While working towards accomplishing a task, the mind may tell the person to give up, but with persistence, the individual can push through the doubt and achieve the goal at hand.

Almost all successful individuals in history who amassed considerable wealth did so because they had to; there was no other option. Their previous lifestyles were extremely poverty-ridden, and their families depended on them. These ambitious individuals wanted to experience the good qualities of life. They were not going to take no for an answer; they were going to get rich or die trying. No matter what barrier stood in their way, their sense of persistence was too powerful to allow failure.

The quality of possessing overwhelming persistence is irreplaceable. The individuals who have mastered the act of persistence live life on their terms, with a piece of mind that displays happiness and control. No matter the situation, no matter how many times these individuals are met with temporary setbacks, they know they will accomplish the task as long as they do not give up.

If doubt creeps into the reader's mind while reading this chapter, analyze anyone living a successful lifestyle. There are millions of testimonies illustrating the trials and tribulations these now successful individuals had to overcome. These people are who they are because they did not give up; they did not stop believing in their purpose. They truly believed that they were placed on this earth to make a difference, and through persistence, they did just that. They were rewarded for not giving up, to the point where they are now praised, looked up to as role models, and some have positively affected millions of people's lives worldwide. Do not give up; success is right around the corner.

CHAPTER 10

POWER OF THE MONEY-MAKING TEAM

In this chapter, we will go over the importance of an organized money team. For this text, a *money team* can be defined as two or more individuals working towards a common goal in a spirit of complete agreement. Countless individuals have accomplished great success by utilizing a money team. Financial gains become a high possibility for the individual who incorporates themself with a competent group of people who open heartedly provides guidance, advice, and confidential assistance in a spirit of complete agreement. This kind of collaborative partnership has signified the source of almost every transcendent success story.

The spiritual aspect of the money team principle is difficult to understand because it has a lot to do with spiritual energies. Many individuals do not believe there are energies outside of physical observation, but there is without a doubt a force of intangible energy that dwells among humans.

It is a fact that whenever two or more minds come together, there is generated a hidden, immaterial force that can create another mind, one that is not physically seen but is felt. The reader can apply any personal evaluation of the times when they have tried to figure something out among multiple individuals, and the multiple personalities were operating as one mind. Another example of this principle can be seen in any corporate meeting where the participating individuals attempt to solve relevant problems that can affect everyone involved.

It is incredibly vital for the reader to understand this scientific fact; there are solely two undisputed established elements in the entire world: energy and matter. The recently mentioned statement is relevant because the individual mind is a form of energy. This statement is why two or more individuals' minds regulate a complete agreement spirit; multiple minds combine relevant forms of energy to create an isolated form of thought. A combination of intellects connected in a manner of agreement will produce more thought-energy than an individual mind, just as an assortment of batteries will produce more energy than a singular battery. This reasoning is why the money team concept is essential to the accumulation of wealth.

When multiple people intentionally act in complete agreement with each other while striving for a particular goal, they place themselves in a situation that will allow them to absorb power directly from the universal energy. This schematic action is how the individuals striving for prosperity earn the title of genius.

Every individual who has acquired a vast wealth has recognized the power of surrounding themselves with people who will increase their chances of accomplishing their primary goal. The more people one surrounds themselves with that have the same goals, plans, and ambition, the more likely one will accomplish the objective at hand.

CHAPTER 11

The Importance of Love, Sex, and Romance

The proper application of love, sex, and romance can make any person a highly successful individual. There is no more significant influence on an individual's method of thinking than love and sex. The reader should apply a realistic evaluation of the recently mentioned statement to recognize this truth.

To apply validity to this chapter's introduction, let us discuss the importance of sex in the journey towards thinking and getting paid. If a person wants to develop a wealth mindset, they will benefit significantly from practicing sexual transmutation. Regarding this text, the meaning of sexual transmutation can be defined as altering sexual thoughts into productive thoughts of attaining a desirable objective of choice.

The sentiment of sex has the power to transform a mediocre thought into a thought that manifests genius through transmutation. In other words, a person who takes the idea of sexual expression and applies that desire to achieving relevant goals will attain a productive tunnel-vision state of mind. The reader can find the truth of this statement in the fact that sexual desire is the most influential of all personal desires. When motivated by sexual desire, humans develop sharpness of decision making, courage, willpower, tenacity, and creative ability unfamiliar to them at other times. People who realize this truth and intentionally redirect their need for sexual expression can perform incredible inventive feats in any profession or calling, especially wealth accumulation.

Before an individual attempt to utilize the benefits of sexual transmutation, they must accept that a tremendous amount of willpower will have to be applied. The desire to express oneself sexually cannot and should not be dismissed entirely. Everybody working towards personal achievement should provide this powerful stimulant an outlet through actions that improve a person's body, mind, and soul. If no productive outlet is provided, the person's sexual energy will look for purely physical outlets such as masturbation or sexual engagement with another individual. In other words, if this natural energy is not converted into some creative endeavor, it will find a less reliable outlet.

Extensive scientific research of the sexual natures of humans has revealed that the men and women of notable success possess a high level of sexuality. The previously mentioned statement is believable because, in situations where the person is motivated by sex, they become gifted with a superpower for action. The reader can find the validity of this truth in the fact that the human mind responds to stimuli that elevate thinking to high rates of vibration, identified as enthusiasm, creative imagination, and intense desire. The urge for sex expression is one of the most effective and influential mind stimulants.

A person who learns how to transfer the urge for sexual expression into a productive means of action can achieve a genius level of thinking. Before we go any further, let us first define what a genius level of thinking is. Regarding thinking and getting paid, a helpful definition of a genius is a person who has learned how to enhance their thought vibrations to enable the individual to deliberately communicate with sources of information not attainable through the regular rates of thought vibration.

Genius-level thinking is developed through the faculty of creative imagination. This version of imagination provides the personal connection that links the limited mind of humans to Universal Energy. The reader can find the preceding statement's truth in the countless inventions humans have produced throughout history conceived by ideas or theories flashed into their minds called hunches. These hunches are achieved when the mind is vibrating at a remarkably high frequency. When elevated to this greater level of thought, the individual is not hindered by any stimuli that limit their mental activity. This particular individual is in a state of mind where common thoughts have been wholly excluded, and the mind's creative ability takes over all mental activity. The mind becomes receptive to ideas and concepts that could not enter the individual's mind under different conditions. This version of mental production can be characterized as a genius level of thinking.

The celebrated artists, authors, musicians, and businessmen became renowned because they obtained the habit of relying upon their inner voice, which converses internally through the faculty of creative imagination. It is a truth that individuals who possess perceptive imaginations have their most beneficial concepts through inspirations or hunches. They achieve these high levels of inspiration by stimulating their minds to vibrate at a higher level of frequency, primarily through the practice of sexual transmutation.

Sexual energy by itself is a powerful mind stimulant, but its forces are frequently uncontrollable. This is where the emotions of love and romance come into play. The emotion of love, similar to sexual emotion, is also a powerful mind stimulant. When harnessed positively, it can be the driving force to financial success for the relevant individual. When love starts to blend itself with the passion of sex, the effects can range from the peace of ambition, dignity, the efficiency of judgment, and spiritual perspective.

Love, Romance, and Sex are all emotions that motivate men and women to pursue outstanding accomplishments. Love is the emotion that works to warrant stability, dignity, and productive labor. Romance is the emotion that promotes the qualities or feelings of mystery, thrill, and remoteness within the individual's life. In the situation where these three emotions are mixed, the individual's thought process becomes similar to a genius's thinking approach.

It is vital for the person attempting to think and get paid to encourage loving, sexual, and romantic thoughts and withhold all the negative thoughts no matter how difficult it may be. The mind flourishes upon the dominating thoughts fed to it, whether the thoughts are positive or negative. Through the consistent application of willpower, a person may control any emotion or thought. When a negative thought manifests itself in a person's mind, it can be transformed into a positive or productive thought by the uncomplicated method of switching thoughts.

CHAPTER 12

THE SUBCONSCIOUS MIND

According to Merriam-Webster, the subconscious mind is the component of a person's mind that conveys ideas and feelings but is not immediately available to consciousness. Another way of describing the subconscious mind is a faculty of an individual's consciousness that involves every impulse of thought that enters the objective mind through any of the five senses. The subconscious also collects and registers sense impressions or thoughts, despite their quality. The subconscious is essential to thinking and getting paid because of this faculty's capabilities to transform an individual's idea, thought, or plan into its tangible or financial equivalent. This faculty operates non-stop, day and night. A person cannot completely control their subconscious mind, but they can

intentionally give over any plan, desire, or purpose to the subconscious.

There is an abundance of proof to confirm that the subconscious mind combines a human being's limited intellect and universal energy. In other words, the subconscious is the go-between through which a person may pull upon the capabilities of universal energy on demand. The subconscious alone bears the mystical method by which mental desires are altered and converted into their spiritual equivalent. It is the means through which a person may forward the invocation to the source able to acknowledge prayer.

After the reader has accepted the truth regarding the presence of the subconscious mind and comprehends its potentialities as a means for converting your ambitions into their tangible or financial equal, you will then embrace the importance of exclusively thinking thoughts of prosperity and success. Remember, the subconscious mind operates deliberately, whether you perform an attempt to influence it or not; this implies that feelings of fear and inadequacy and all negative thoughts work as provocations to your subconscious mind unless you subdue these impulses and eliminate all toxic thoughts. If a person fails to direct their mind towards achieving their primary goal, the subconscious mind will gather and file the thoughts that reach it due to negligence.

Everyone reading this text should understand that countless thought impulses influence your subconscious mind without your awareness every day, all day. These impulses come in all types of varieties, some negative, some positive. Every person must try their best to negate the negative impulses and deliberately influence their subconscious mind by seeking positive notions related to accomplishing their primary goal. These actions will allow the individual to unlock the full potential of their subconscious mind.

If the reader is having difficulty understanding the importance of the subconscious regarding the obtainment of financial wealth, let us place the entire concept in perspective. It is a fact that anything a person creates or invents initially begins in the form of thought vibration. Following the thought vibration, through the assistance of the imagination, the thought vibration is then assembled into plans or ideas that could induce satisfactory achievement in one's preferred vocation. After the thought vibration is transferred through the imagination and combined with faith, the subconscious takes over the process and converts the thought into its tangible equivalent.

The subconscious mind is more responsive to thought vibrations combined with high levels of feeling or emotion, no matter the variety of feelings or emotions. The thought vibration can be positive or negative; as long as an influential feeling is mixed with the thought, the subconscious will do its best to grant a tangible realization of the thought.

With the recently mentioned statement in mind, all readers of this text should become accustomed to the more basic emotions. Regarding this text, we will cover seven primary positive emotions and seven influential negative emotions. The positive emotions that all readers of this text should seek are the emotions of desire, faith, love, sex, enthusiasm, romance, and hope. There are other positive emotions, but the recently mentioned emotions are the most influential and most regularly utilized when performing various creative endeavors. Understand these emotions by application, and the other positive emotions will be at your request when you require them. The negative emotions that are to be avoided are fear, jealousy, hatred, revenge, greed, superstition, and anger.

It is a scientific fact that positive and negative affects cannot occupy the mind simultaneously. It is up to the individual to decide which variety of emotions will dominate their brain.

The individual also must ensure that the positive emotions legislate all influence of the mind. These actions are vital because the occupancy of a singular negative in the conscious mind is enough to ruin all possibilities of valuable guidance from the subconscious mind.

CHAPTER 13

THE BRAIN

For the sake of this text, let us think of the human brain as having a characteristic similar to a radio station regarding the vibration of the thought process. Within the faculties of the ether, each human brain can accumulate thought vibrations that are released by other brains. The concept of the brain being a receiving set entails the brain's capability to receive thoughts released by others' brains, just like that same brain can deliver thought vibrations to others.

This particular transmitting and receiving method occurs when the mind is stimulated to a high rate of vibration. This straightforward stimulated process occurs when the individual's thoughts are combined with feelings; these feelings can be either positive or negative. Sexual emotion is the most influential feeling regarding the stimulation of thought. Sexual transmutation, in particular, increases thought vibration to the point that the person's creative imagination comes to be profoundly receptive to ideas, which it accumulates from the ether. When the brain is vibrating at an accelerated frequency, it does not solely attract thoughts and impressions released by other brains through the medium of the ether. Still, it allows one's thoughts to become revved up in a manner that thoughts instantly influence one's subconscious mind. The broadcasting principle represents the mental process of combining feelings or emotions with thoughts and transferring those thoughts to the subconscious. The operation of an individual's cerebral transmitting process is a relatively straightforward method.

Even though every human being owns a brain, the comprehension of the brain's capabilities is a mystery to many people. Regarding the purpose of this text, all one needs to understand about the brain is its intangible capabilities. The brain is the mental headquarters where thoughts go to work in an extraordinary attempt to translate thoughts into their tangible equivalent. Once an individual understands this concept, that individual will achieve anything they desire.

CHAPTER 14

Intuition

The following principle we are going to discuss is intuition. Through the proper application of utilizing one's intuition, the individual can receive guidance from the universal energy on demand.

This particular principle is among the most essential, beneficial, and spiritual principles of the whole think and get paid philosophy. The topic of intuition is controversial because of its intangible characteristics. Intuition can be wholly learned, comprehended, and implemented by mastering the other wealth-building principles mentioned throughout this text. Intuition originates in the part of the subconscious mind defined as creative imagination. This particular faculty of the mind is where innovative concepts, strategies, and thoughts flash within cognizance. These flashes are termed hunches or revelations.

Comprehension of the capabilities regarding intuition occurs particularly by meditation through consciousness development from within. Intuition is the intermediary of the relationship linking humans and Universal Energy, the apex at which the mind of man communicates with Universal thought.

Through the guidance of intuition, the individual will be alerted of threatening hazards in time to evade them and informed of opportunities in time to encompass them. Intuition has the capabilities to provide the individual an abundance of wisdom and knowledge that can be drawn upon whenever the person desires. By applying the teachings of this text, the reader may influence this unlimited intelligence portal to assist in transforming aspirations into tangible form.

The author realizes that this part of the text includes a subject with which most people are not familiar. The capability of intuition is a topic that commands tremendous interest and profit to the individual whose purpose is to amass significant funds. However, the topic of intuition may not interest the people who desire nothing more than a life of mediocrity and security. As mentioned earlier in this chapter, the benefits of the incredible power of intuition develop gradually by implementing the other teachings described in this publication. It does not matter what your overall purpose is for reading this text; all that matters is the reader realizes that they do not have to settle for anything in life that is undesirable, but there is complete control of all circumstances in their lives by utilizing the great gift from the universal energy which is their mind.

This analysis of intuition was included in this think and get paid text because it is intended to give a comprehensive philosophy by which the readers of this book may confidently and efficiently guide themselves to accomplishing whatever they demand of life. At the beginning of this text, the author presented the origin of all achievements being embedded in an intense desire to achieve a specific goal. At the end of the text, the author provides the necessary principles needed to take that desire and translate it into a variety of knowledge that leads to a comprehension of oneself, of other people, of the rules of life, perception, and understanding of what is required to become truly happy.

Furthermore, eventually, by reading and acting on the principles presented in this book, the reader will find themselves in ownership of a skill that will allow them to dismiss any variety of discouragement, control fear, defeat procrastination, and embrace their creative capabilities. When this happens, the reader will be in the same mindset as countless geniuses, innovative thinkers, artists, musicians, writers, business people, and any other person of outstanding achievement. At that moment, the person will truly understand the unlimited possibilities of transforming any desire into its tangible or monetary equivalent as quickly as the individual can think and get paid.

CHAPTER 15

HOW TO OVERCOME NEGATIVITY

We have now arrived at the conclusion of this text. Before we go into the final principle, the author wants the reader to give themselves a much-deserved pat on the back. Because of your dedication and desire to change your financial freedom, you are now in possession of the most effective skill any man or woman may ever desire, the knowledge to know that your mind can help you achieve anything you want in life. Any person in possession of this knowledge can now live a life of peace and happiness without any worry in the world. Now we can analyze the various forms of negativity that will attempt to attack your mental insecurities. There is a tremendous difference between wanting to do something and doing it. Initially, an individual who has learned the principles mentioned would want to go out in the real world and be this tremendous success. Even though this particular activity is very much possible, it will by no means be easy. A believer of the concepts mentioned in this text will be constantly faced with potent negative influences.

The ambitious person will have to accept the recently mentioned statement as truth and prepare their mind for the impending mental war. Preparation to participate in the battle of your mind entails a comprehensive awareness of the negative influences and how to destroy those opposing forces.

These negative influences are the notions of poverty, criticism, ill health, old age, and death. There are various other negative influences, but they are most likely categorized under the previously mentioned influences. These forces are solely states of mind that can be directed or controlled with a conscious effort.

Before we detail these negative influences, we should remember that an individual's thought vibrations will always be translated into the thoughts' tangible equal; it does not matter whether those thoughts are relatively positive or negative. Therefore, to win the inevitable mental war, the individual must recognize that each human can effectively regulate their mental impulses. This truth, united with the supplementary truth that every person has the power to change thoughts of negativity into thoughts of self-belief and courage, provides a sufficient weapon that will destroy this mental enemy. Now let us examine the different varieties of negative influences and how to eliminate these mental enemies.

The negative notion of poverty is one of the leading mental influences and why so many people go through life struggling financially. As mentioned throughout this text, if somebody wants to achieve financial freedom, they must understand that a wealth mindset attracts favorable finances, and a poverty mindset attracts poverty.

Anyone who demands wealth must initially decide how much money will constitute financial freedom and what actions will be needed to acquire that quantity of money. Actions demonstrating self-doubt and worthlessness will hinder wealth acquisition, and no one will blame the relevant individual. The obligation of outwitting the negative thoughts of finances is yours because the ambitious person is the only person that has the power to change the thoughts of poverty into thoughts that demand adequate compensation.

The mental influences of poverty are only thought impulses that attempt to creep into a person's mind; this particular influence has little to no power. Only the individual can keep those influences from dwelling in their mental capacity. Poverty influences particularly become relevant when the individual allows it to dictate conscious processes.

It is essential not to allow poverty influences to win the mental battle because a poverty mindset is enough to derail any possibility of accomplishment in any endeavor. A poverty mindset diminishes the faculty of judgment, impairs the faculty of creativity, abolishes self-confidence, weakens enthusiasm, hinders ambition, creates confusion of primary goals, inspires procrastination, and makes intrapersonal discipline impractical. A poverty mindset sabotages the chance of rational thought, makes concentration extremely difficult, discourages tenacity, clouds long and short-term memory, and summons failure in each imaginable way possible. A poverty mindset hinders friendships, attracts all sorts of stress, restlessness, anxiety, and sadness. All of the mentioned consequences can be eliminated if the individual accepts that they dwell in an environment of extraordinary abundance, with nothing standing between their economic, emotional, and spiritual achievements but the negative mental influences.

The influences of a poverty mindset are unquestionably, the most unfavorable of the negative mental influences. The consequences of a poverty mindset are the most challenging to conquer because it demands a substantial amount of courage to defeat this particular mental enemy. Poverty is something countless ambitious individuals have had to overcome throughout history, and if the reader wants adequate wealth, they also have to overcome this negative influence. This mental enemy can be defeated quickly with the proper dedication, and a life of financial freedom can be experienced.

The subsequent negative influence the driven individual will have to defeat is the fear of criticism. According to the Oxford dictionary, *criticism* is the expression of dissatisfaction with someone or something based on observed deficiencies or errors. This negative influence hinders countless numbers of individuals from attempting or completing all types of endeavors.

The anxiety a person obtains while being concerned with the criticism of others can be highly damaging because of its capabilities of eliminating initiative, discouraging creativity, and undermining any belief in self-reliance. This particular negative influence is one of the most potent enemies of mental freedom, mainly because of its unfavorable impacts on the ambitious person's self-consciousness, dignity, temperament, initiative, and enthusiasm.

It is essential for the individuals who wish to live a life of prosperity and happiness to not worry about other people's criticisms. The only opinions that should matter to the ambitious person are the opinions coming from the people within their money-making team. It does not matter if it is family, friends, associates, or coworkers; if they are not contributing to your overall purpose in life, their opinions and criticisms should not be of any importance.

The following harmful mental enemy that will have to be defeated on the battlefield of the mind is the influence of ill health. An individual who is always worried about being sick or unhealthy will never have mental freedom. The author understands that sickness and disease are actual issues, and many people have suffered various health-related problems. However, the constant worry of ill health is the mental enemy that will derail any chance of significant personal achievement.

One of the main reasons the worry of ill-health is so damaging is that the person who constantly believes they have some form of disease or sickness will inevitably produce the tangible symptoms of the disease feared. The recently mentioned statement is true because of the powerful capabilities of the mind. As we examined throughout this text, the mind will produce the tangible manifestation of the ideas and thoughts constantly conveyed to the subconscious. The conveyed ideals of an ill-health mindset must be transmuted into good health ideals, for this is the only way this particular negative influence can be defeated. Without sound health, any chances of personal achievement are slim to none.

The subsequent negative influence that can derail anyone's chance of success is the fear of old age. This particular negative influence carries the possibility of preventing the infected individual from genuinely enjoying life, live a life of paranoia, and many other undesirable circumstances.

The fear of old age brings distrust of every person the individual may encounter, the ungrateful action of not genuinely being satisfied with any tangible goods they may acquire during their lifetime, and not eagerly awaiting the most significant years of life. The self-belief stating something is wrong or depressing with growing old is exceptionally toxic to the subconscious mind. This particular worry has become such an intrapersonal issue that countless individuals have over time become concerned with the ill effects of poor health regarding old age, along with being extremely reluctant to believe in themselves sexually. The ambitious individual can overcome these negative thoughts by focusing on their goals and overall purpose in life. When those thoughts come into your mind, one must instantly suggest that only positive benefits result from aging. Knowledge and wisdom are now the individual's unstoppable weapons that can be used on the battlefield of the mind. There is abundant evidence proving that a human being improves mentally, emotionally, romantically, and spiritually, especially between forty and sixty.

Out of all the negative influences, the most common of all is the constant worry of death. Death affects every person living and is something everyone will have to encounter at one time or another. The recently mentioned facts are what causes so many individuals to worry about death constantly, and this consistent worry can affect the ambitious person's method of thinking and derail any chances of significant personal achievement.

The uncontrollable worry of death, in many ways, is the most destructive of all the primary negative influences. One of the main reasons this negative influence affects so many people is the dilemmas of death caused by religious fanaticism. Many religious people are worried about their souls being transferred to some post-death environment such as heaven or hell or whatever their specific religion states their souls will go after death. These beliefs can cause numerous individuals to act out to indicate where they believe they are going after death. They ignore everything life has to offer and only concern themselves with what will happen after death. The rationale that proves the constant worry of death is a waste of time dwells in the fact that no person truly knows what happens after death. Fear of death is worthless, and death will come regardless of what anyone may believe about it. It is far more beneficial to the subconscious mind to accept death as something in which there is no control of and commence to enjoy the life given to the fullest extent possible.

Now that the main negative influences have been analyzed let us examine the actions that will need to be taken to protect ourselves against these negative influences. The first and primary rule regarding protecting oneself against negative influences is to realize that you possess the ability to control your mind and willpower. With the use of this internal willpower, the individual can put it to use in any situation in which there is a need to build a wall of immunity against negative influences in your mind or outside influences.

The ability to recognize that the mind is under the absolute control of the individual that possesses it is the best way to overcome negative influences. This statement is the most meaningful and encouraging of every fact comprehended to man. If the individual fails to control their mind, they will endure a life susceptible to one or all of the negative influences mentioned earlier in this chapter. Total control of the mind is not easy by any means; it results from the consistent practice of self-discipline and productive habits.

Another technique anyone can use to hinder negative influences and effectively control the mind is deliberately keeping their mind busy by performing acts that complement the attainment of their definite purpose. The analysis of countless successful individuals proves that they have achieved the level of achievement they did by mastering this technique. Successful people deliberately take full command of their minds; moreover, they apply specific actions and concentrate on accomplishing particular goals. Without this mental command, success is not plausible.

In conclusion, before reading this text, the reader may have had a valid excuse for not living a life of happiness, prosperity, and peace of mind. Now that the reader has thoroughly read this text, that excuse can be dismissed. This dismissal is because the reader now understands that the mind can give the individual anything they want as long as specific actions are taken to accomplish their detailed goals. There is no punishment for writing down goals, possessing a burning desire to reach those goals, and applying definite action to achieve these goals. All it takes is for the individual to believe they can achieve anything they want in life; in other words, all it takes is for the individual to think and start getting paid.

About the Author

The author, Evie Lawson, is a United States Marine Corps veteran. After serving two combat tours in Afghanistan, Evie was honorably discharged from the Marine Corps. Despite the various unfavorable circumstances derived from a difficult transition into the civilian world, he began the decade-long journey of researching the most successful individuals in hopes of discovering how they amassed the wealth, fame, and achievement they possessed. After analyzing numerous books, biographies, videos, interviews, and relevant texts, Evie was able to organize all of the information gathered and construct an easy-to-read book called "Think and Get Paid," detailing the tips, techniques, and strategies utilized by five hundred of the world's most successful individuals. Mr. Lawson has a bachelor's degree in Real Estate Studies, a bachelor's degree in Entrepreneurship, and a master's degree in Business.

Book Description

What is Think and Get Paid about?

Think and get paid is a simple, straightforward statement, yet these words are powerful enough to change anyone's life who believes and acts on its message. Earth provides a large abundance of evidence proving that energy directed towards a specific goal inevitably manifests itself into realization. It is an undeniable truth that "the mind is the most powerful tool man has at their disposal." A human being can literally think and get paid or whatever else they may desire to acquire. The author wrote this book for individuals who believe that success leaves clues and inquires to understand the actions and thought patterns that made millions of people successful throughout history.

www.ingramcontent.com/pod-product-compliance
Lightning Source LLC
Chambersburg PA
CBHW071844290426
44109CB00017B/1921